FROZENBIRD

Lila & Luna
THE KIND BOOKS

Written by
JASON DOLLERY

Illustrated by
SANJA ČEŽEK

To our kindest girls, Eliza & Luna.

In the bleak mid-winter
the forest falls quiet.

Under a blanket of snow
all creatures take comfort.

In the warmth of their fur all
prey huddle together; for
there is safety in numbers
all must remember.

Yes, there are hunters on the prowl
who have sharp teeth that bite.
With eyes that can see the smallest of trembles
in the darkest of nights.

Even as I say this,
a hunter is in search of their next meal.
So stay safe in your bed and hope you don't become
the next scream, whimper or squeal.

Now a hungry wolf in the winter
is brave, quick, and keen.
He can kill - then vanish
without a single track left at the scene.

But a wolf is not without a heart,
although the winter makes it cold.

Behind his sharp teeth and claws,
he is still the same cub his mother
would love, sing to, and hold.

One day, a wolf picked up a trail -
it was faint, but it was fresh.
So he stalked a little closer
expecting movement or warm vapored breath.

To his surprise, laid a bird;
frozen, weak and still
with a sprig of berries
stretching from its tail to its bill.

In that moment he remembered
a scene from long ago
when he was little younger
and collapsed from exhaustion in the snow.

He gave up all hope,
tears had filled his eyes
as he thought about his mother
and wished they said goodbyes.

In his last moments
a shape scurried slowly, yet ever-near.
A young curious rabbit who knew better,
but overcame her fear.

She offered her sprig of berries
expecting nothing in return.
Or, perhaps, maybe that kindness
is the gift we all must learn.

Jumping back to the present,
our wolf knew this bird must be saved;
picking up its feathered body
and running quickly to his cave.

Our wolf became a guardian,
patient and calm.
As the bird began to thaw,
our wolf had done the opposite of harm.

The bird regained his strength
and awoke to quite a fright -
a hunter with big teeth
was holding him rather tight!

Please don't eat me sir!
I am a skinny little bird.
We taste rather nasty
in case you haven't heard?

Today is not your last,
my scrawny little friend.
I plan to take you home
and reunite you with your kin.

As the prey and hunter journeyed,
the bird broke the winter's silence with a song;
a tale about a wolf,
who passed a lesson of kindness along.

So you see my dear reader,
life is not just black and white.

Hunters can be kind
and even the smallest of prey
can have the strongest of might.

Sanja & Jason are currently working on their new book.
If you loved "Frozenbird", please keep an eye out on:

MOONGOOSE

Few words about LilaLuna Publishing

From the deepest, darkest forests, to the tallest, windswept peaks - empathy and kindness find a way to inspire the very best that humanity has to offer.

Our goal is simple. We create stories that offer wonder, kindness and compassion to the children who read them, so that when their adventures unfold, they're equipped with tools to be their own inspiration.

Find out more: www.lilalunapublishing.com

www.ingramcontent.com/pod-product-compliance
Lightning Source LLC
Chambersburg PA
CBHW042106090426

42811CB00018B/1863